PREACHING:

The Centrality of Scripture

R. Albert Mohler

THE BANNER OF TRUTH TRUST

THE BANNER OF TRUTH TRUST
3 Murrayfield Road, Edinburgh EH12 6EL, UK
PO Box 621, Carlisle, PA 17013, USA

*

© The Banner of Truth Trust 2002
First published 2002
Reprinted 2012

ISBN: 978 0 85151 823 7

*

Typeset in 11/15 pt New Baskerville
Printed in the USA by
VersaPress, Inc.,
East Peoria, IL.

PREACHING:
The Centrality of Scripture

I would ask that we think seriously and soberly about the task of preaching. As we do so, I would direct us to the text of Scripture, to 2 Timothy 4:1–5.

I solemnly charge you in the presence of God and of Christ Jesus, who is to judge the living and the dead, and by His appearing and His Kingdom: preach the word; be ready in season and out of season; reprove, rebuke, exhort with great patience and instruction. For the time will come when they will not endure sound doctrine; but wanting to have their ears tickled, they will accumulate to themselves teachers in accordance to their own desires; and will turn away their ears from the truth, and will turn aside to myths. But you, be sober in all things, endure hardship, do the work of an evangelist, fulfill your ministry.

Thus Paul charges Timothy, in strong language, regarding the importance of preaching. And so the Word of God confronts us as we attempt to think biblically about our task in proclaiming the Word. As we survey the church, it would seem that preaching is in a state of crisis.

A CRISIS IN PREACHING

Now at the outset we might admit that the word *crisis* is certainly one of the most overused terms in our contemporary vocabulary. Yet the intentional use of the term by many contemporary observers does indicate some urgent unease, some conscious concern, and some heartfelt reflection upon the state of preaching in the churches today.

If there were a crisis of preaching, what would the distinguishing marks of such a crisis be? How would we recognize this crisis? By dropping attendance in the churches? By decreased attention in the pew? By the declining cultural appeal of preaching? Perhaps by the declining social status of preachers? Or might the reality be far more devastating than this?

Might the true evidence of a crisis in preaching be instead immature and even ignorant Christians falling prey to false doctrine? Or a worldly church proclaiming an increasingly worldly message? Or confusion and secularity? Or a lack of discipline in our churches? Or the development of factions and factionalism?

Perhaps such a crisis in preaching cannot be quantified statistically at all. What if such a crisis were more fundamentally evidenced by the substance of what we preach or fail to preach?

Second Timothy is Paul's valedictory address to the church. It is also his charge to Timothy, his young protégé in the ministry. As later verses indicate, Paul knew that he was coming to the very end of his ministry. He testified that he had fought the good fight, he had finished the race, he had kept the faith. He held his example before Timothy for the aspiration and emulation of the younger minister. His words carry great weight because we know this is Paul's last word to the church, the last message he expected to deliver to Timothy, and, beyond Timothy, to the church.

Obviously, Paul had invested very high hopes in Timothy. We know from the New Testament that Paul's relationship with Timothy developed over quite a long period of time, and it involved very direct tutelage and modelling. *Second Timothy* contains a chastening word for all of us, perhaps along these lines: Is there anyone into whom we have poured ourselves, into whom we are pouring ourselves, into whom we are willing to pour ourselves, as Paul poured himself into Timothy, and gave himself to Timothy?

We see in this text the weight of Paul's self-consciousness in the presence of God as he addressed himself to Timothy in these words: 'I solemnly charge you in the presence of God and of Christ Jesus, who is to judge the living and the dead, and by His appearing and His kingdom.' I don't know about you, but if I were Timothy, all it would take to get my attention would be the name of Paul. All that it would take to arrest and command my attention would be knowing that the letter I held was a message from Paul.

But Paul here says that this word is not merely Paul's word. It is from God. It is addressed to Timothy in the presence of God and of Jesus Christ Himself, this One who will come to judge the living and the dead, who is Lord and Sovereign over His own Kingdom. 'It is in the presence of God and Christ Jesus that I charge you, preach the Word. Preach the Word!'

THE CONTEXT

The overall context of this passage is found, of course, in the entire epistle of Second Timothy. But its particular context is found in the turn that takes place in chapter 3, verse 14. In describing to Timothy problems in the church, and in giving Timothy, as it were, a diagnostic tour of what to beware of in the church, and in identifying those whom he should oppose, Paul writes in very strong language of rebuke.

But in verses 14–17 there is a striking transition as Paul says, as it were, 'But you':

> You, however, continue in the things you have learned and become convinced of, knowing from whom you have

learned them; and that from childhood you have known the sacred writings which are able to give you wisdom that leads to salvation through faith which is in Christ Jesus. All Scripture is inspired by God and profitable for teaching, for reproof, for correction, for training in right-eousness; that the man of God may be adequate, equipped for every good work.

'But you.' This is quite a significant turn, and one that I am quite certain must have come as a great warning and, at the same time, as a great solace to Timothy. After all these warnings about those who would cause injury to the church, Paul comes to Timothy and says, 'But you.' 'You, however, your ministry must be faithful, your attitude higher, your commitment weightier. Continue in the things you have learned, knowing from whom you have learned them.' We will recall that Paul clearly taught that there is a succession of faithful teaching. He taught Timothy to commit these things to faithful men, who would teach yet others (*2 Tim.* 2:2). A succession of faith-ful teaching is Paul's concern. And he reminds Timothy, not only of those things which he has learned, but of those from whom he has learned them.

But then comes the primary issue. The primary teacher in Timothy's life has not actually been Paul. It has been the Holy Scriptures. Since childhood, he has known the Holy Scriptures. And Paul writes eloquently, passion-ately, and pointedly about the authority, power, and truthfulness of the Bible. The immediate reference in this letter from Paul to Timothy is the Old Testament, and the apostolic testimony. Paul used the Greek word *graphe* to describe the words of Jesus as well as the Old Testament Law, Wisdom Literature and Prophets. Now we understand and confess that *graphe* refers to the entire canon of Scripture, the sixty-six books of the Old and New Testaments. These are the Holy Scriptures – the inspired, infallible, and inerrant Word of God, the Bible.

This passage contains rich promises. We are promised that this Word is profitable for teaching, for reproof, for correction, and for training in righteousness. Furthermore, we are informed of a purpose behind Scripture: that the man of God might be complete. This can be properly translated also as 'adequate' or 'mature'. The promise of the Scriptures is to make the man of God thoroughly furnished, completely furnished, finished, equipped, and completed unto all good works.

THE CHARGE

Therefore, Paul says, know what you have been taught. Hold fast to the deposit of faith. Know by whom you have been taught. And know most fundamentally that it is the Holy Scriptures which have been your guide and your teacher and are presently your authority. Know all this, and as Paul solemnly charges Timothy, 'Preach the Word.' He is to preach the gospel, the Word of light. He is to preach the truth of the gospel. He is to preach the whole of the gospel. He is to preach the purity of the gospel. He is to preach the power of the gospel. He is to preach no other gospel.

This solemn charge means that we must preach the Word. We must preach it in season and out of season. We must preach the Scriptures. Paul clearly and unbreakably links the Word, that is, the gospel, with the written Word, that is, the *graphe* – the Scriptures.

The link between the preaching of the gospel and the preaching of the Word is indissoluble and unbreakable. Nevertheless, the sad history of the last two centuries indicates an increasing pattern of preachers who attempt to 'liberate' the gospel from the Scriptures. This pattern we must condemn.

As evangelical preachers, let us commit ourselves together to the preaching of the Word. Let us confess together our dependence upon the Bible as the Word of God written. We know that the Scriptures are our authority. This is the Word addressed to us; these books of the Old and New Testament are our authoritative text, our witness, the deposit of faith.

Paul wrote these words to Timothy, and yet, as Sidney Greidanus has suggested, our need is even more urgent than was Timothy's because, unlike Timothy, we do not have the Apostle Paul.[1] We do not have direct contact

[1] Sidney Greidanus, *The Modern Preacher and the Ancient Text* (Grand Rapids: Eerdmans, 1988), p. 8.

with an apostle. Our need is even more urgent and direct than was Timothy's. Our dependence is more comprehensive. We are heralds, not originators. We are charged to preach a message we have received – not to invent a message that will be well received. We are to preach that which has been sent, delivered, and addressed to us, not a message that has been developed or altered. Greidanus continues with this admonition:

> Accordingly, if preachers wish to preach with divine authority, they must proclaim these messages of the inspired Scriptures, for the Scriptures alone have divine authority. If preachers wish to preach with divine authority, they must submit themselves and echo the Word of God. Preachers are literally to be ministers of the Word.[2]

We are to be servants of the Word. We are not Lords over the Scriptures. We are servants of the Word. We should not be embarrassed to say so, to preach so, and to live so. Indeed, if we are embarrassed to preach the Word, we will do grave injury to the church. We will be a millstone around the neck of the church, an evil shepherd misleading the flock and leading them to disaster.

Paul's very simple and direct imperative is this: 'Preach the Word.' Preaching is itself a Scripture-founded event and moreover, as John Piper has suggested, a Scripture-

---

[2] *Ibid.*, pp. 12–13.

saturated event. From its beginning to its end, we are to preach the Word. We are to preach no other Word. Preaching cannot be severed from Scripture, if it is to be authentic Christian preaching. There is the temptation in many modern pulpits to separate Scripture from preaching, but in the Christian church this must never be so. Sometimes putting Scripture in its most simple form speaks the truth most directly. J. I. Packer has suggested, in short, that preaching is 'an activity of letting texts talk'.

It serves as a reminder that a central part of our purpose as preachers – as heralds in preaching the Word – is to get out of the way. We are not to put ourselves into the text, but to get ourselves out of the way of the text. The purpose of preaching is not that we ourselves might be heard, but that the text of the Word of God might be heard. We preach, not that we might impress or be impressive, but that the Word of God might makes *its* impression on the human heart.

A REVOLT AGAINST SCRIPTURE

Clearly, not all agree. There are those who, as Paul warned, preach messages designed to satisfy 'itching ears'. We live in the midst of a generation of itching ears, with a self-centred focus, pervasive individualism, subjectivism, relativism, and deadly spiritual sickness. The cause of this apostasy is deeply spiritual. We now see a revolt against God and a revolt against God's Word. Here we face the stark reality of our crisis in preaching – a revolt against Scripture. On the liberal wing of Protestantism, we see an increasing rebellion against Scripture and distance from Scripture.

Two witnesses will make this case with clarity. The first of these is Professor Edward Parley of the Divinity School of Vanderbilt University. Dr Parley celebrates what he calls 'the collapse of the house of authority'.[3] No authorities such as Scripture, he suggests, have any place in the post-Enlightenment world. He makes clear his rejection of both the truthfulness and the authority of Holy Scripture. The Bible, he says, is marked by error, corruption, oppression, and other evils. Authentic preaching, he suggests in a recent article in *Theology Today*, should at times indeed preach *against* Scripture. He states his case straightforwardly: 'The Christian church is summoned to the apostolic task of preaching the good news, and to preach biblical passages is to reject that summons.'[4]

Interestingly, he taunts preachers who reject the inerrancy of the Scripture, but who continue to preach biblical texts. These are his words:

> We must pose a question. Given a rejection of biblical inerrancy and the acceptance of historical-critical

[3] Edward Parley, *Ecclesial Reflection: an Anatomy of Theological Method* (Philadelphia: Fortress Press, 1982), pp. 165–6.

[4] Parley, 'Preaching the Bible and Preaching the Gospel', *Theology Today*, 51 (1994), p. 100.

methods, what is the basis of the claim that something preachable is necessarily in the text? Why is a word or truth of God necessarily present in a passage of the Bible chosen by a lectionarist or by the preacher? Such an assumption seems more arbitrary and more incoherent than the fundamentalist view. But why would someone who thinks that the Bible originated historically, contextually, and editorially, thus reflecting the human and even corrupted perspectives of its writers, think that any passage one happens to select must contain something in or about it that is proclaimable?[5]

Rarely do we see such candour. Seldom do we see such a direct and unvarnished rejection of biblical authority and such an unembarrassed demand that preaching must be severed from the biblical text. Tragic though this is, Dr Parley is at least honest.

A similar word comes from his Vanderbilt colleague, David Buttrick, one of the most influential homileticians of our day. Buttrick, whose father was an eminent preacher in the mainline churches during the middle of the twentieth century, directs his charge against biblical preaching with these breath-taking words: 'For the better part of the twentieth century, preaching and Bible have been wrapped up in a kind of incestuous relationship.'[6]

---

[5] *Ibid.* [6] David Buttrick, *A Captive Voice: The Liberation of Preaching* (Louisville, Kentucky: Westminster/John Knox Press, 1994), p. 9.

Consider those words – 'an incestuous relationship'. The cold chill of spiritual death blows by as these harsh and horrible words take shape. His candour is breathtaking. His arrogance is thunderous. Preaching and the Bible, said Dr. Buttrick, are fundamentally incompatible. How does he understand Scripture? These are words from his book, *A Captive Voice: The Liberation of Preaching:*

> So what does the Bible offer? The Bible rolls out myth and winds up in eschatological vision. What the Bible offers is narrative with an elaborate mythic beginning – creation and fall, Cain and Abel, Noah's ark, the tower of Babel. And, in the last chapters of Revelation, drawing on Ezekiel, we are offered eschatology – a Holy City with grand visions of consummation. So the Bible offers meaning – not in every little passage; some Bible passages may be largely irrelevant or even sub-Christian – the Bible offers meaning by handing out a story with a beginning and an end and, in between, a narrative understanding of how God may interface with our sinful humanity.[7]

Now just imagine if Paul had communicated to Timothy with this understanding of the Scripture. Perhaps it would have sounded like this: 'All Scripture is problematic and some is sub-Christian, but nonetheless profitable for myth, eschatological vision, narrative understanding and interface with our humanity.' No

[7] *Ibid.*, p. 17.

[14]

hope, no truth, no authority, no gospel! Thanks be to God, we hear Paul as a counter-voice, commanding and exhorting the faithful church without apology, 'Preach the Word!'

We cringe and flinch and we are repelled when we hear the Bible rejected and impugned and maligned. We would say to ourselves, 'Surely evangelicals preach the Word. Surely as those who confess the infallibility, authority, inspiration, and inerrancy of Scripture, certainly we preach the Word. We preach it in season and out of season.' But I wonder if actually we are as faithful as we imagine ourselves to be. In listening to much evangelical preaching I am led to wonder if it is actually gospel, biblical, scriptural preaching at all.

Sociologist Marsha Whitten has recently written *All Is Forgiven*. Her book embodies the findings of a major research project tracing sermons preached by both mainline and evangelical Protestant preachers, including an enormously large sample of Southern Baptist ministers. The sermons were all based on Luke chapter 15, and the Parable of the Prodigal Son. Dr Whitten's work is fascinating and very alarming. What she found is that even though evangelical preachers give great lip service to the authority and inspiration of the text, their sermons often quickly depart from it and descend to lesser concerns.[8]

[8] Marsha Whitten, *All is Forgiven: The Secular Message in American Protestantism* (Princeton: Princeton University Press, 1993).

BIBLICAL IGNORANCE

Among liberals, the Bible's authority and inspiration are often rejected and thus the Scriptures are largely absent. But among evangelicals, even though the Bible's authority and inspiration are confessed, the Scriptures are often soon abandoned. Evangelicals are so easily seduced and co-opted by the surrounding culture. The Bible is often displaced by the authority of our personal experience, programmatic concerns or pragmatic goals.

Research indicates widespread biblical ignorance among evangelicals and, I fear, even among Southern Baptists. We find ourselves immersed in a consumer culture the likes of which the world has never seen. Around us lies an entertainment culture in which the pulpit seems misplaced. We see ourselves pressed by a marketing mentality, not only in the larger world, but also in the church itself. We see ourselves confronted with congregations who want quick how-to messages addressing their personal concerns.

Research suggests that increasingly the pulpit discourse, preaching, and sermons of evangelicals concern themselves primarily with the constellation of issues which revolve around the self rather than with the universe of meaning which comes from the Holy Scripture. This is a chastening word to us. We should be reminded this morning that the Reformers' principle of *Sola Scriptura*, the formal principle of the Reformation, was intended to guard the church lest it turn to tradition, human authority, or the *magisterium* of the church, as a word which would compromise the authority of Scripture. It is Scripture alone which the church should hear.

Evangelicals at the end of the twentieth century are quite immune from the danger of subservience to an ecclesial *magisterium*. Our individualism and our anti-authoritarian posture have taken care of that. The greater danger for us is that we listen not to a *magisterium* above, but to the inner child, or whatever seems to be the voice within. It is not so much the danger of tradition that threatens *Sola Scriptura* in our midst, as the lure of the therapeutic, of the technical and the marketable.

IN SEASON AND OUT OF SEASON

Paul says we are to preach the Word in season and out of season. And what a fascinating word-play that is, as Dr A. T. Robertson pointed out. It is a play on the Greek word *kairos*. Paul exhorted Timothy that he is to preach the Word *eukairos* and *akairos*, in season and out of season. Thus, we are to preach when it seems an opportune time and when it looks like anything but an opportune time.

We have underestimated, I submit, what Paul meant when he charged Timothy to preach the Word in season and out of season. We sometimes act as if it means when it's popular and when it's not – when it is in vogue and when it seems out of date. I don't think this sums up the substance of Paul's concern. I think Paul's concern lies

[17]

far deeper than this. Paul is not merely concerned with popular taste and cultural trends. Far more deeply than that, Paul means, by 'in season and out of season', when it fits and when it does not fit, when it works and when it seems not to work, when it bears visible fruit and when it seems barren, when it is appreciated and when it is denounced, when it is legal and when it is illegal, when it is plentiful and when it is scarce, when it is broadcast on airwaves and when it is preached in catacombs. We are to preach the Word at all times.

Paul commanded that, 'in season and out of season', we are to preach. And we are to preach the Word so that we convince, rebuke, and exhort. He used several imperatives in his charge to Timothy. *Preach* the Word, and then *convince*, make the case for the faith, defend the gospel. *Rebuke*, correct error, be bold to say what you know, on the basis of Scripture, to be true, and confront where falsehood is present. Furthermore, *exhort*, urge, and encourage the church to righteousness.

There is authentic passion here, a deep passion which comes from Paul's heart to Timothy and pulsates from the text of Scripture to us. For the time will come, Paul says, when they will not endure sound doctrine. He warns Timothy the time will come when preaching will be out of vogue and out of season, and instead itching ears will look to be tickled and scratched.

Preaching is such a high calling, the responsibility weighs so heavily on us, the yoke is upon all who would stand in the pulpit to preach, to *preach the Word*. We must make Scripture central, as our authority. It is the Scriptures which bear witness of Christ (*John* 5:39).

Professor John A. Broadus, founding Professor of Homiletics at the Southern Baptist Theological Seminary, believed fervently in the power of preaching. Even in Broadus' generation, some suggested that preaching might become outdated; that it might be replaced by the printed word. Broadus responded in these terms:

> When a man who is apt in teaching, whose soul is on fire with the truth which he trusts has saved him and hopes will save others, speaks to his fellow-men, face to face, eye to eye, and electric sympathies flash to and fro between him and his hearers, till they lift each other up, higher and higher, into the most intense thought, and the most impassioned emotion – higher and yet higher, till they are borne as on chariots of fire above the world, there is a power to move men, to influence character, life, destiny, such as no printed page can ever possess.[9]

'Our business', he taught his students, 'is to teach God's Word. Our task is to set forth what the text contains.' Dr Broadus added: 'To interpret and apply his text in accordance with its real meaning, is one of the

[9] John A. Broadus, *A Treatise on the Preparation and Delivery of Sermons* (Philadelphia: Smith, English and Co., 1870), p. 18.

preacher's most sacred duties. He stands before the people for the very purpose of teaching and exhorting them out of the Word of God.'[10]

Just recently I came across the very last words that Dr Broadus ever taught in the classroom. While conscious of his approaching death, he finished his teaching career at Southern Seminary by teaching a Thursday class in the English New Testament. After reviewing it, he turned to his students and decided to depart from his lesson plan. These are the words, as recorded by a student in the class.

'Young gentlemen, if this were the last time I should ever be permitted to address you, I would feel amply repaid for consuming the whole hour in endeavoring to impress upon you these two things, true piety and, like Apollos, to be men "Mighty in the Scriptures".' Then pausing, he stood for a moment with his piercing eye fixed upon us, and repeated over and over again in that slow but wonderfully impressive style peculiar to himself, 'Mighty in the Scriptures', 'Mighty in the Scriptures', until the whole class seemed to be lifted through him into a sacred nearness to the Master. That picture of him as he stood there at that moment can never be obliterated from my mind.[11]

[10] *Ibid.*

[11] Cited in A. T. Robertson, *Life and Letters of John Albert Broadus* (Philadelphia: American Baptist Publication Society, 1901), p. 430.

Never again was Broadus to set foot in the classroom at Southern Seminary. In a matter of days, he lay on his deathbed. Like Paul, his exhortation remains. 'Be "mighty in the Scriptures".'

Paul's final words to Timothy ring in our ears:

'Preach the Word in season and out of season.
Preach the Word!'

Note: This address was originally delivered as a convocation message to the Southern Baptist Theological Seminary, Alumni Memorial Chapel, 30 January 1996.

The Banner of Truth Trust originated in 1957 in London. The founders believed that much of the best literature of historic Christianity had been allowed to fall into oblivion and that, under God, its recovery could well lead not only to a strengthening of the church today but to true revival.

Inter-denominational in vision, this publishing work is now international, and our lists include a number of contemporary authors along with classics from the past. The translation of these books into many languages is encouraged.

A monthly magazine, *The Banner of Truth*, is also published and further information will be gladly supplied by either of the offices below or from our website.

THE BANNER OF TRUTH TRUST

3 Murrayfield Road
Edinburgh, EH12 6EL
UK

PO Box 621, Carlisle
Pennsylvania, 17013
USA

www.banneroftruth.org